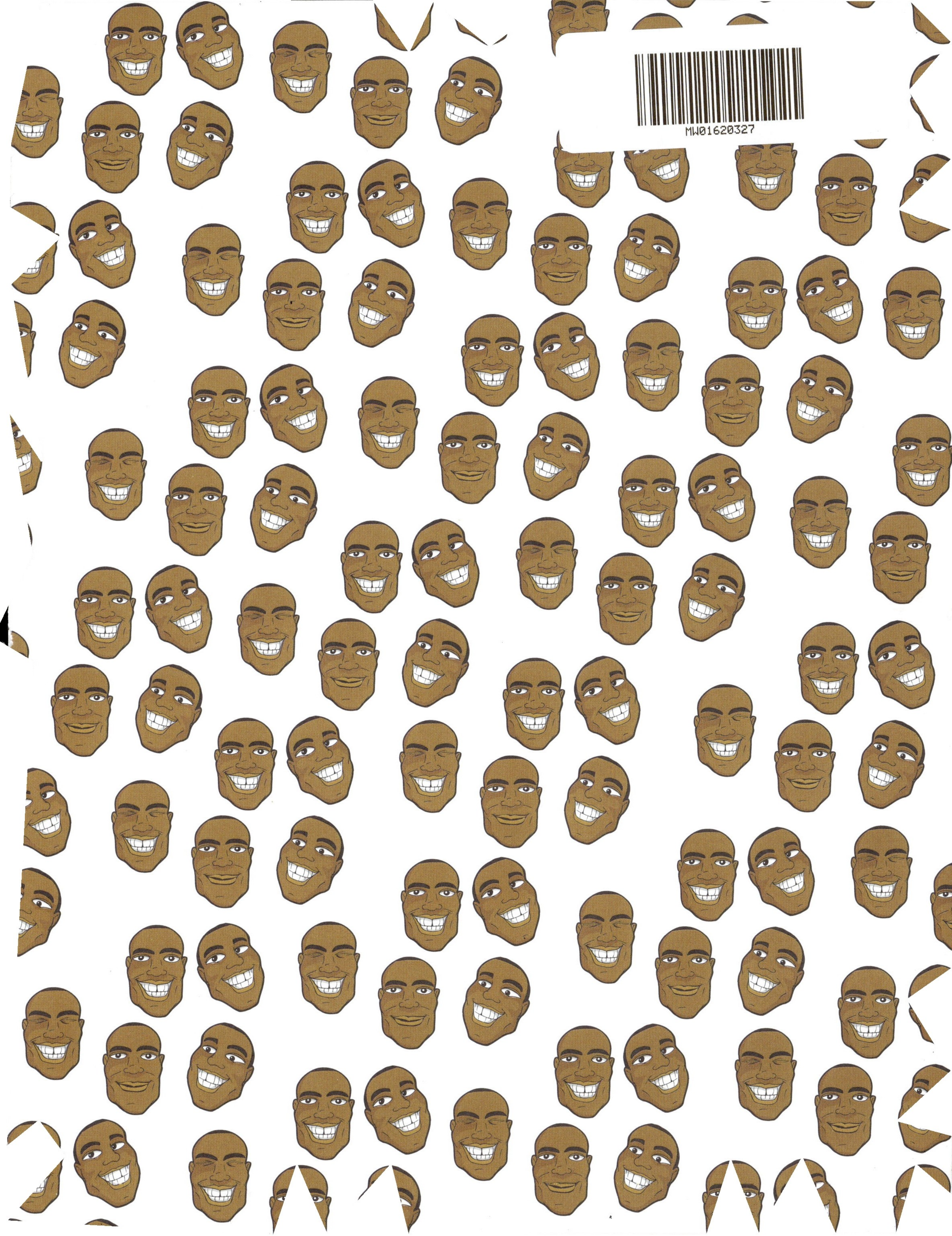

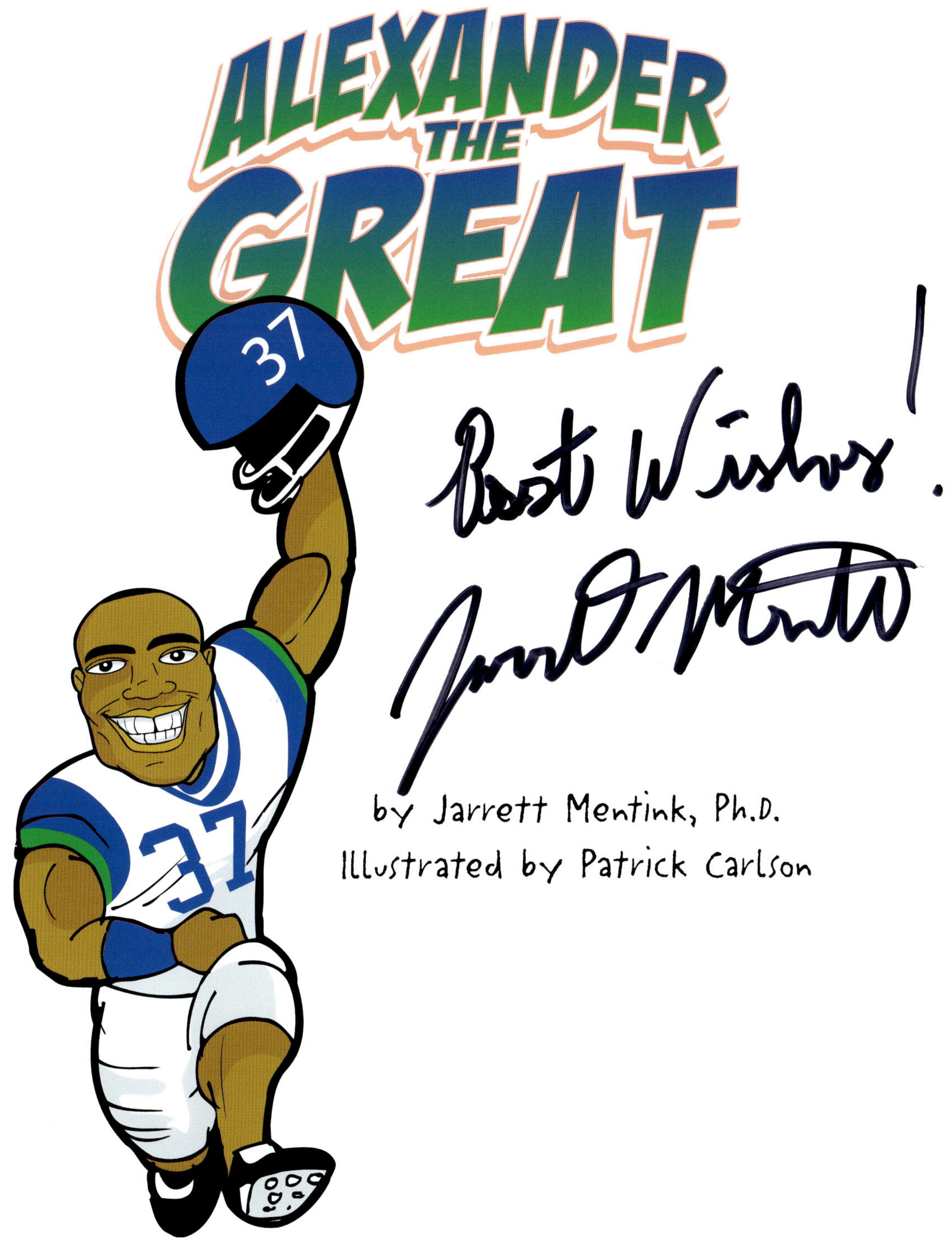

This book is dedicated to all of those parents who help their kids to fly!

Printed in Korea, First Edition.
ISBN: 0-9723314-1-7

Published by Kids in the Clouds™
www.kidsintheclouds.com

Have you heard the stories
of Heroes and Kings,
Of wonderful feats
and mystical things?

Well most of these tales
like dragons are past,
But I know of one
whose legend grows fast!

This is a tale

that takes place in Seattle,

Of a great warrior

who leads Seahawks to battle!

He challenges Giants,

Raiders and foes,

And on every Sunday

his legend grows.

He wears on his chest
a three and a seven,
And runs by the rest
as if sent down from Heaven.

But illusion he's not,

for this hero's real.

His name's Alexander

and football's his deal!

He runs like the wind
and his legend is grand.

He's the best running back

in all of the land!

He once had a game

where he scored 5 T.D.'s!

And best of all,
his team won with ease!

Yes, Shaun is a hero,

but not for his play.

Shaun is a hero

because of his way.

His way is of goodness,

kindness and care.

His mom taught him early

it's important to share.

Born in Florence,

a town in Kentucky,

He was blessed with great talent

but hard work made him lucky!

He went on to star

at Boone County High,

Making sure of his grades

to keep his limit the sky.

He chose Alabama
and never broke stride,
Setting all kinds of records
and chanting "Roll Tide!"

Once again he worked hard

to get his degree.

He knew it would lead him

to the top of the tree!

Then came the draft,
first round in the pros!
He worked even harder
to stay ahead of his foes!

He made sure he was ready

so when he got the chance,

He'd score bundles of touchdowns

and let the fans dance!

While others were napping

and playing around,

Shaun kept on working

to keep his game sound.

So when they decided to

give Shaun the ball,

He ran over Giants

one hundred feet tall!

He trampled on Steelers

and stiff-armed those Bucs.

When Shaun gets the ball,

they all cry “Aw-Shucks!”

Now there've been many teams
and many great players,
Like Emmitt and Barry,
and of course ol' Gale Sayers.

But the thing about Shaun
that makes him unique,
He's a gamer on Sunday
but he's special all week!

He has a foundation

to help those in need.

He gathers with children

to teach them to read.

To put it quite simply,

with this soaring Hawk,

When it comes to his values,

he walks the walk.

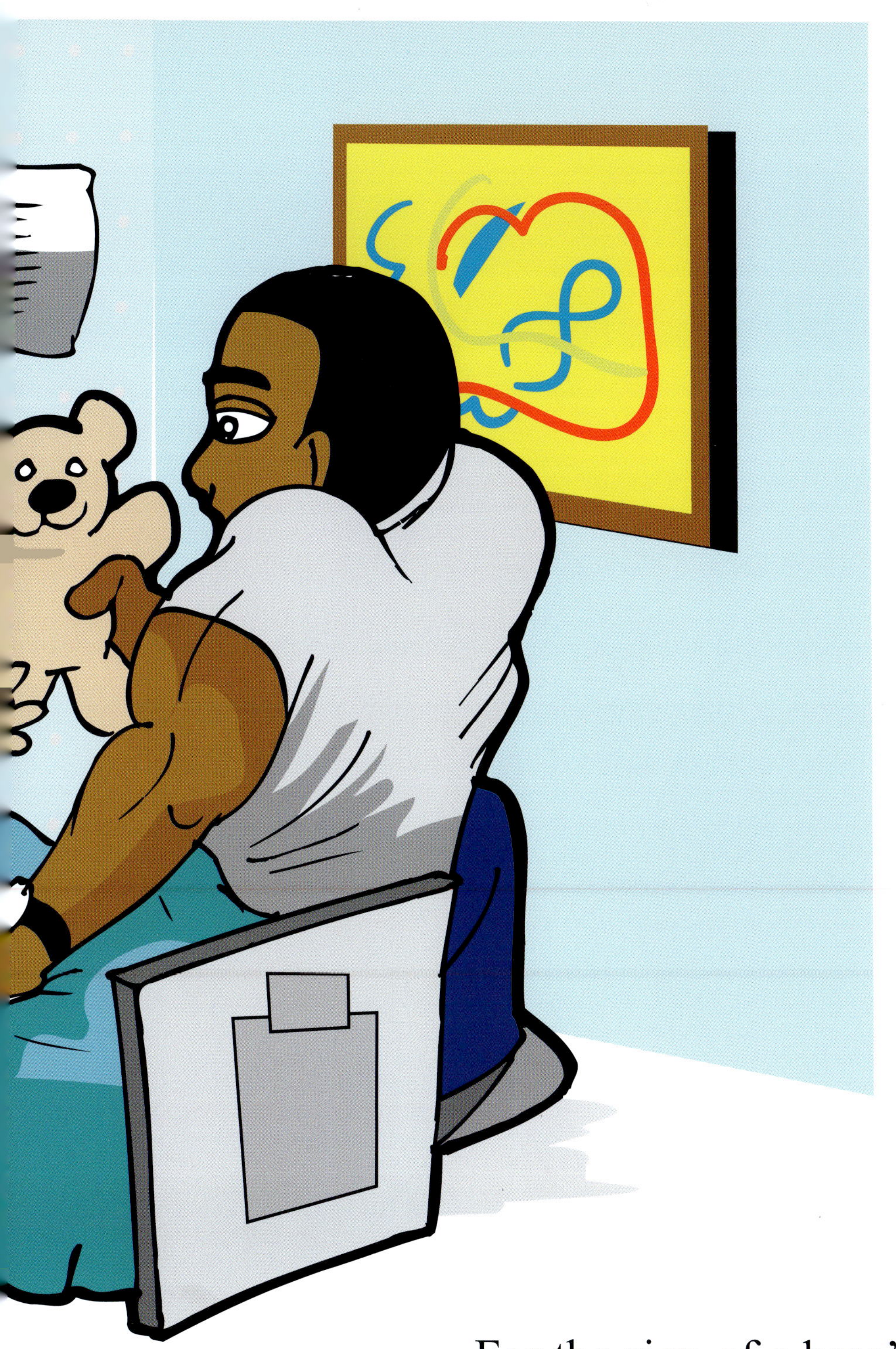

For the sign of a hero's
not the records they stack.
The sign of a hero
is what they give back!

Like all great heroes

Shaun is much more —

A bright shining star

with an incredible core!

For more on Shaun and his involvement in the community, check out his website at www.shaunalexander.com.

Patrick Carlson began his cartooning career in 1990 when he began creating designs for a local screenprinter. Since then, he has developed thousands of cartoon characters and illustrations for businesses and websites all over the world. Patrick lives in Valdosta, GA, and more of his work can be seen on his website, www.hotspotgraphics.com.

37
37